CCSS **Genre** Folktale

MW00570381

Essential Question
What choices are good for us?

The Weaver of Rugs

A Navajo Folktale

retold by Lana Jones • illustrated by Francisca Marquez

Chapter 1

Searching for Help

Once, the Navajo people didn't know how to weave. Sometimes it was too cold to collect plants or hunt animals. The people became weak and hungry. They didn't have enough to eat.

Two women wanted to help their people. They decided to ask the **wise** ones for help. The wise ones lived far away.

The women set off on their journey. They became lost, and they called out, "Help! Please someone help us!"

STOP AND CHECK

Why did the women go on a journey?

A woman **appeared** on a cliff above them. She wove a strong web. She threw the web over the women. Then she pulled them up to the top of the cliff.

"I am Spider Woman. What do you want?" she asked them.

"Our people are cold and hungry," said one of the women. "Can you help?"

"I will help," said Spider Woman. "But you must do what I tell you."

Spider Woman broke off thick branches from a tree. She used them to make a frame. She wound her special threads up and down the frame.

"You can use this loom to weave," she said.

STOP AND CHECK

How did Spider Woman make the loom?

6

Chapter 2

Learning to Weave

The women were **confused**.

"How will a loom feed our people?" they asked.

"Watch what I do," said Spider Woman.

Spider Woman wove another web. She threw it over some sheep. She showed the women how to cut the wool off the sheep. Then she made the wool into yarn.

"Our people can't eat yarn," said one of the women.

"Do you want me to help you?" Spider Woman **interrupted**.

She helped the women make dyes from leaves and berries. She told them how to dye the yarn. Finally she taught them how to use the loom to weave a rug.

"Do the best you can. Don't be careless and make mistakes," Spider Woman said. She went away.

The women worked for days. They became fast, **graceful** weavers. But they couldn't figure out how weaving would help their people. They thought Spider Woman wasn't helping them. They got angry and left holes in the rug on purpose.

STOP AND CHECK

Why were the women careless with the rug?

Chapter 3
Finding the Answer

At last, Spider Women came back.

"We have finished the work," one of the women told Spider Women.

"Now we **expect** you to help our people," said the other one.

"This rug isn't perfect! Go home," Spider Woman said. "Think about what I have shown you."

The two women were sad. But they wanted to help their people. So they went home and taught their people how to weave. They showed the people all the things that Spider Woman had shown them.

STOP AND CHECK

What did the two women show their people?

13

The people wove rugs for their families and friends. They created beautiful **patterns**. The rugs kept them warm. The people made more rugs than they needed. They traded extra rugs for food and other goods. They became healthy and happy. At last, the two women figured out how Spider Woman had helped them.

The women cooked a **flavorful** meal to thank Spider Woman. They took the food to the place Spider Woman lived. The **luscious** **aroma** **drifted** around the cliffs.

"Spider Woman, where are you?" they shouted.

They called and called, but Spider Woman never came.

The Navajo people became famous for their weaving. The two women never saw Spider Women again. They wondered if she had ever **existed** at all.

STOP AND CHECK

How did the two women try to thank Spider Woman?

Respond to  Reading

Summarize

Summarize the main events of this story. Use your chart if you wish.

Details

↓

Point of View

Text Evidence

1. Reread page 14. What does the narrator think about the Navajo women? Point of View

2. Find the word *careless* on page 8. What does it mean? What clues help you figure it out? Vocabulary

3. Write about how this story would be different if Spider Woman had told it. How would she have described the two Navajo women?

Write About Reading

Compare Texts
Read about making paper mats.

How to Weave Paper Mats

The skill of weaving has been around for a long time. People weave baskets and rugs. You can weave a paper dinner mat.

What You Need:

- two pieces of colored paper, each 12 inches long and 9 inches wide

- ruler

- pencil

- scissors

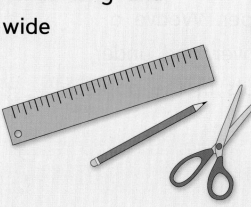

17

What to Do:

1. Fold one sheet of paper in half.

2. Draw a line that is 1 inch from the edge.

3. Make even-spaced cuts up to the line.

4. Take the second sheet of paper. Cut strips that are 9 inches long and 1 inch wide.

5. Unfold the first sheet of paper. Weave a strip over and under the cuts in the paper.

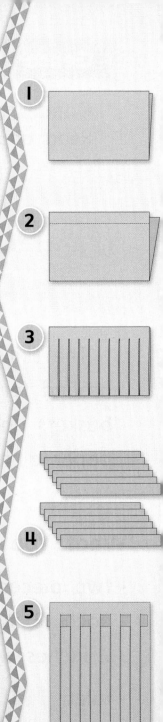

6. Weave the next strip through the paper. Swap the order when you go over and under.

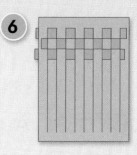

7. Keep weaving the strips. Be sure to swap the order each time.

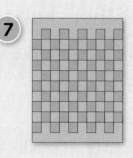

Use a **variety** of colors for your mats. Enjoy the **healthful** food you can eat on them!

Make Connections

How has weaving helped people in the past? Essential Question

The women in the story wove rugs. You can weave dinner mats. What other things do people weave?

Text to Text

Focus on

Genre

Folktales A folktale is a story that has been passed from one person to another. Folktales are not real. Some folktales give us information about the real world.

Read and Find *The Weaver of Rugs* is a folktale with a character that can do magical things. In real life, the Navajo people are skilled weavers.

Your Turn

Work with a partner. Find examples in the story where Spider Woman does magical things.